'DAT LITTLE PLANTATION COOKBOOK

RECIPES BY REMY LATERRADE
ILLUSTRATION AND TEXT BY JOSEPH ARRIGO

A Certified Product Of Louisiana

COVER PHOTO: REMY LATERRADE
PAGE DESIGN: SUSIE AYO
PRINTING ACADIANA PRINTING

© Copyright 1995 by

**P.O. Box 3942
Lafayette, La 70502-3942**

ISBN 0-9632197-4-X "Library of Congress Catalog Card Number" 95-068416

All rights reserved. No part of this publication may be reproduced or transmitted in any form by any means, electronic or mechanical, including photocopy, recording, or any information storage or retrieval system, without permission in writing from the publisher, except by a reviewer who wishes to quote brief passages in connection with a review written for inclusion in magazine, newspaper, or broadcast. Chef Remy has published this cookbook in order to make available one of the styles of delicious Cajun cuisine that can be prepared with familiar condiments and ingredients. Those ingredients that are not available in your area can be obtained by writing to: Remy Laterrade, P.O. Box 3942, Lafayette, LA 70052-3942, for information about local inspected and approved supplies.

All recipes have been tested by the editor, but differences in meat types, oven and stove temperature, cooking utensils, and availability of necessary ingredients must be considered in all instances of success and failure. Every attempt has been made to keep the recipes simple, yet complete.

While this cookbook reflects a time of rich plantation heritage, the recipes proximate to specific plantations are not necessarily indigenous to that particular plantation. Rather, recipes reflect much of the times and certainly the flavor of the time surrounding the era itself. The cookbook is a sharing of quality pen and ink reproductions of some of the fine plantation and recipes. It is not designed to be an exact reflection of history other than as it affects our time now.

❧ DEDICATION ☙

THIS BOOK IS DEDICATED FIRST AND FOREMOST
TO OUR LORD JESUS CHRIST
WITH WHOM ALL THINGS ARE POSSIBLE.

IT IS ALSO DEDICATED
TO THE PEOPLE OF SOUTH LOUISIANA.

✎ ABOUT THE AUTHOR ✎

Remy Laterrade was born in New Orleans. He has been cooking since he could reach the stove (about age 8 or 9) and has been cooking ever since.

He apprenticed under Chef Rene, later taking over the kitchen and running the restaurant for one year. After that time, he finished his first cookbook which he began writing while living among the Cajun people of Lafourche parish. While having a working knowledge of Cajun and Creole cooking, when in Lafourche parish he began to learn the home style versions of Louisiana's best Cajun recipes. He is still active in professional food preparation and catering. He also does many Cajun and Creole food demonstrations throughout the South.He is presently a member of the American Culinary Federation and is working on further accreditation.

✍ ABOUT THE ARTIST ✍

Joseph A. Arrigo is a noted New Orleans author, artist and illustrator. Topics of the books he has authored and/or illustrated range from New Orleans, to Louisiana and Mississippi Plantation homes, to the Mississippi Gulf Coast

His illustrations have won many awards in shows throughout the south. Prints of many of his illustrations are also sold in most historic home and museum gift shops in Louisiana and Mississippi.

◦◦ TERMS TO UNDERSTAND ◦◦

BISQUE   Is a thick spicy soup, usually with a cream base and some meat or seafood.

BLACKENED   To fry a season-coated piece of meat or fish in butter on a very high
              temperature until black in color.

CAJUN TRINITY Chopped onion, bell pepper and celery.

CARAMELIZE   To saute' onion, bell pepper and celery in butter until moisture is gone and
              vegetables begin to brown.

ETOUFFEE'   To "etouffee" is to smother with onions and other vegetables (Usually
              bell pepper and celery).

FRICASSEE	To cook meat or fowl in butter and then in a seasoned liquid.
GRILLADE	Thinly sliced strips of meat (usually pork) that are pan fried.
GUMBO	Basically a Cajun soup that has a roux base.
JAMBALAYA	Everything mixed together and cooked in one pot, with rice and stock, and cooked until rice has absorbed almost all liquid.
PANNE'	To fry a breaded or floured meat in a small amount of oil on high heat. This is usually done in a cast iron skillet, but any skillet will do.
REDUCE	To bring to a boil, and through evaporation reduce the amount of water to concentrate the essences in a less diluted mixture.

(CONTINUES)

ROULADE   Rolled meat or poultry.

ROUX   Roux is simply a mixture of oil or butter and flour. There are three basic rouxs for cooking. The white roux which is used in white sauces and for simple thickening. The tight (or medium roux) is a paper bag colored mixture used for thickening and flavor. Finally there is a dark roux that is used primarily for color and flavor. (Instructions to follow)

STOCK   Water that has been enriched by boiling parts of meat and/or vegetables until the essence of the parts has become a part of the liquid. Always strain stocks and skim fat to assure a pure and lo-cal source of flavor and nutrition.

∞ CAJUN MEATS ∞

ANDOUILLE Usually a large diameter sausage that is made up of pork and seasoning that is smoked until completely cooked. Used in gumbos and jambalayas.

SMOKED SAUSAGE Cajun smoked sausage is similar to most smoked sausages except that it is usually more highly seasoned and smoked with a variety of wood from hickory to pecan or oak.

TASSO Tasso is a very lean, thinly sliced pork that is highly seasoned and smoked to perfection. Tasso can be used as a meat source or as a type of seasoning to enhance vegetables or sauces.

☙ The Roux ❧

White Roux The white roux is simply butter or margarine and flour. This is the base of white sauces, cream sauces and white or sawmill gravy. It is made by melting butter and adding flour and blending completely. In this case there is usually more butter than flour. I recommend for every tablespoon (15ML) of butter you add 1½ tablespoons (23ML) of flour.

Tight Roux The tight (light brown or medium) roux is used primarily to thicken, although it is flavorful as well. This is made with either butter or oil and flour (although I recommend butter). Equal parts of butter and flour are used to achieve this roux. Melt butter (or heat oil) and add flour. Whisk together and continue on medium high heat until mixture thickens and becomes a paper bag brown color.

DARK ROUX   The dark roux is possibly the most used roux in Creole/Cajun cooking. There are several opinions about the color of a dark roux. I use a very dark colored roux (about the color of dark chocolate) and have a definite style of preparing it. Most say to mix equal amounts of oil (do not use butter, use an oil that can stand up to high heat, i.e. peanut oil or canola), and flour, but as you become familiar with the process I suggest you increase the flour by about 20%.

HOW TO COMPLETE THE DARK ROUX

It is essential that you understand the importance of a successfully completed roux. Since it is an integral part of many Creole/Cajun recipes you must not scorch or burn the roux. When you first begin to make a roux you will experience a very distinctive smell. In fact, the completed roux will have a slightly burned flour smell. If you follow the instructions to the letter you will not burn the roux. You must use patience in this process. If you are not patient you will surely burn the roux or will not achieve the desired color. Once you have mastered the process, this smell will become pleasant to you and all in your household, because the smell means something good is coming from the kitchen.

Heat oil to slightly hot. Add flour and blend with the utensil of your choice (most people say a wooden spoon, some use a metal spatula, I use a wire whisk). YOU MUST WHISK OR STIR THE MIXTURE, CONSTANTLY SCRAPING THE BOTTOM AND EDGES UNTIL ROUX IS COMPLETED! Keep on high heat until flour begins to brown. When the oil begins to smoke you must reduce heat to medium or medium high (depending on your skill) and continue to whisk or stir until the roux gets to a dark brown color. At this stage you can do a couple of things. You can remove the roux from heat and stir until the roux the roux before you reach the desired color. It will progress to a darker color because of the heat that is retained in the oil. The other option is to remove from heat when the roux is almost the color you want and add chopped fresh onion to the hot roux and stir until the onions stop steaming. (CAUTION! THE STEAM FROM THE ONIONS WILL BURN YOU IF YOU ARE NOT CAREFUL). I use the latter method.

◆ SUGAR ◆

The agricultural economy of South Louisiana was changed forever in 1795 with the successful production of granulated sugar from boiling cane juice by plantation owner Etienne deBore. In 1822, Jean J. Coiron introduced steam-power to the milling of sugar, and sugar became the major crop of the many plantations along the state's bayous and rivers. Crops of indigo and tobacco were abandoned for the lucrative growing of sugar cane.

Though cotton was the other major crop grown in Louisiana, most of the plantation homes shown in this book were built from the wealth created by sugar

❧ RECIPE INDEX ❧

∽ Plantation Index ∾

❧ Foreword ❧

This book is a culmination of two art forms. Cooking, along with pen and ink reproductions of some of the plantations seem to be a great combination. This is particularly true when it comes to Louisiana cooking and art.

While the recipes are not necessarily particular to the plantations they accompany, the recipes selected are a reflection of the popular Louisiana favorites. This should provide the user with a broad reflection of Louisiana culture to use and to share with others.

The recipes are top notch, quality offerings that will give the cook the information needed to complete quality Louisiana dishes. The pen and ink will serve as a short guide through at least one segment of the architectural magnificence associated with Louisiana's history.

✥ DESTREHAN PLANTATION ✥

Located several miles above New Orleans, Destrehan was built in the late 1790's by Robert deLongy. The property, later acquired by his son-in-law, Jean Noel Destrehan, has borne his name ever since.

Indigo, corn and rice were the plantation's first crops, but as most of the plantations along the Mississippi River in south Louisiana, sugar became the predominant, money-making crop.

Architecturally, Destrehan manor house began as a West Indies styled structure, but the addition of garcionierres on both sides of the original building, and a remodeling in the Greek Revival style by a later owner, changed it to it's present appearance.

Destrehan, now owned, operated and continually being restored by the River Road Historical Society, is open to the public on a daily basis.

ꙮ Dark Roux ꙮ

Dark Roux Recipe Accommodates:
For Gumbo: 1 quart liquid
For Stew, or Fricassee': 3 cups liquid
For Gravy: Color and flavor; 1 quart liquid
For thickener: Not recommended

¼ CUP + 1 TBSP	VEGETABLE, CANOLA, OR PEANUT OIL
½ CUP	ALL-PURPOSE FLOUR

Heat oil to hot on high heat and add flour. Whisk until smooth and blended well. If mixture is a little thick it is alright to add a little oil, but keep it to a minimum. Continue to whisk constantly until flour begins to smoke a little. Reduce heat to medium and continue the process until flour mixture is dark brown in color (about the color of dark chocolate).

Remove from heat and continue to whisk for 2 minutes. Reserve for use.

To combine roux with liquid successfully, heat liquid to boiling and add roux a little at a time until completely blended. Boil until mixture just begins to foam or scald, (similar to but not exactly milk). Reduce heat and continue the cooking process of the chosen recipe.

❦ RICE ❧

I GET SO MANY COMMENTS ON RICE COOKING THAT I WILL GIVE YOU ONE METHOD OF COOKING PERFECT RICE EVERY TIME. THIS RECIPE WILL PROVIDE YOU WITH A FIRM AND SEPARATE FINISHED PRODUCT. TRY THIS METHOD AT LEAST TWICE TO GIVE THE METHOD A CHANCE TO WORK FOR YOU.

1 CUP	RICE, LONG GRAIN OR PAR-BOILED*
2 CUPS	WATER, OR FOR A FLAVOR CHANGE, ADD YOUR FAVORITE STOCK
1 TSP	SALT

*You may recognize converted rice as the retail name for par-boiled rice.
Bring water, or stock to a rolling boil. Add salt and stir. Add rice and stir well. Bring back to a boil, stir, cover and reduce heat to lowest setting. Set timer for 20 minutes. When timer goes off, remove from heat, uncover and serve. That's it!

✑ CREOLE/CAJUN SEASONING ✑

USE ONLY DRIED SEASONINGS

1 CUP	SALT	½ CUP	GRANULATED GARLIC
2 TBSP	CAYENNE PEPPER	¼ CUP	ONION POWDER
¼ CUP	BLACK PEPPER	1½ TBSP	CELERY SEED

In a food processor add salt and cayenne pepper. Process for 30 seconds. Add black pepper, granulated garlic and process another 15 seconds. Add remaining ingredients and process another minute. Store in air-tight container. Use for gumbo, jambalaya, etouffee or for your regular cooking. You can also use like salt at the dinner table. Makes about 2¼ cups.

✼ MAGNOLIA MOUND ✼

Located on a natural ridge in Baton Rouge near the Louisiana State University campus, Magnolia Ridge stands majestically as an early example of Louisiana Plantation architecture. It was built in 1791 to serve as a residence for the 1000 plus acre plantation which was part of a Spanish land grant.

The house, which has a colorful historical past, was saved by the Foundation for Historical Louisiana from destruction after a stalwart and legal battle. This noble foundation has restored, preserved and furnished the house and opened it to the public for tours. Interesting, open-hearth cooking demonstrations are given on a regular basis.

❧ Chicken Okra Gumbo ❧

3 WHOLE	CHICKEN FRYERS
3 QUARTS	WATER
1 CUP	VEGETABLE OIL
1½ CUPS	ALL-PURPOSE FLOUR
2 CUPS	ONION, CHOPPED
1 CUP	BELL PEPPER, CHOPPED
½ CUP	CELERY, CHOPPED
3 CUPS	OKRA, SLICED IN ½ INCH CIRCLES
3 TBSP	PARSLEY
2 TBSP	SALT
½ TBSP	CAYENNE PEPPER

In a 6 quart pot, boil chicken until completely cooked, about 45 minutes. Remove chicken and allow to cool. Strain and reserve stock. When chicken is cool, pick meat and reserve. Remove oil from stock and let stand at room temperature. Prepare all vegetables as directed.

In a 6 quart pot, heat vegetable oil on high and add flour. Whisk in well and continue to whisk until mixture begins to brown. Reduce heat to medium and continue to whisk until mixture is a dark brown (about the color of dark chocolate).

Add onion, bell pepper, and celery and stir until sizzling subsides to a simmer. Add okra and stir in well. Mixture will be thick and will need continuous attention for 3-5 minutes. Next, slowly add stock, stirring and blending constantly until all stock is added. Mixture should be soupy in texture. Bring to a rapid boil, reduce heat to low and simmer for 5 minutes. Skim off all oil. Add parsley, salt and pepper. Stir well and simmer for 20 minutes. Add picked chicken and simmer another 15 minutes. Serve over cooked rice.

✧ THE COTTAGE ✧

Construction of this rambling cypress house was begun in 1811 by Thomas Butler III on a 360 acre Spanish land grant. The house features a long gallery across it's front and back with a gabled roof and four dormer windows in front. Many of it's original outbuildings remain and the house is rich with fine furniture and original accouterments. The lovely grounds contain the family cemetery.

The Cottage is operated as a bed-and-breakfast inn in the St. Francisville area where it is located. One of the Cottage's slave cabins was used in the filming of the award winning television movie "The Autobiography of Miss Jane Pittmann".

∽ SHRIMP ETOUFFEE ∾

1 LB LARGE	SHRIMP, UNPEELED WITHOUT HEADS
4 CUPS	WATER
¼ LB	BUTTER
1 CUP	ONION, CHOPPED
½ CUP	BELL PEPPER, CHOPPED
¼ CUP	CELERY, FINELY CHOPPED
2 TBSP	GARLIC, MINCED
1 TBSP	FRESH PARSLEY, CHOPPED
½ TBSP	WHOLE THYME, DRIED
	SALT AND PEPPER TO TASTE
2½ TBSP	ALL-PURPOSE FLOUR
½ TSP	TURMERIC
½ CUP	GREEN ONION, CHOPPED

Peel and reserve shrimp. Put peeling into a 2 quart pot with 4 cups water and boil for 30 minutes. Strain stock and reserve. In a large skillet melt butter on high heat.

Add onion, bell pepper, celery, garlic parsley, thyme, salt and pepper and saute' until onions begin to wilt. Add flour and stir in well. Flour will stick slightly. Continue to stir until flour begins to brown. It will achieve a paper bag or slightly lighter color. Add 3 cups reserved shrimp stock a little at a time and stir well until all is added and well blended. Simmer on medium low heat for 10 minutes.

Add turmeric and stir well. Add shrimp and stir well. Simmer until shrimp are pink and tender (about 7 minutes). Serve over cooked rice topped with fresh chopped green onion.

❧ L'Hermitage ❧

Located three miles North of Burnside, The Hermitage features massive Doric columns and wide galleries surrounding the brick-between-posts construction of this elegant mansion. It was built in 1812 by Michel Bringier for his bride, Louise Aglae duBourg de St. Colombe. The Bringier men fought at the Battle of New Orleans with General Andrew Jackson and the house was named for the General's famous Tennessee Home, The Hermitage.

The house has been beautifully restored in recent years by Dr. and Mrs. William Judice of New Orleans. It is open for plantation tours by appointment.

❧ RED BEANS AND RICE ❧

1 LB	RED KIDNEY BEANS
3 QUARTS	WATER
2 CUPS	ONIONS
1 CUP	BELL PEPPER
½ CUP	CELERY
2 TBSP	GARLIC
1 TBSP	PARSLEY
2 TBSP	SALT
2 TBSP	BLACK PEPPER
1 TBSP	CHILI POWDER
2 LBS	TASSO, JULIENNED, HAM CAN BE SUBSTITUTED

Be sure to have a bottle of TABASCO Brand Pepper Sauce and lots of hot french bread on hand.

Wash beans well then drain. In a 6 quart pot, put beans and cover 3" with water (about 3 qts.). Allow beans to soak for several hours if possible. Chop all vegetables to a fine consistency. After soaking, heat beans on high heat until boiling. Take out ½ of beans and reserve. Add onions, bell pepper, celery, garlic, and parsley. Stir well. Bring to hard boil, reduce heat to maintain boil. Be sure to stir often and add water to maintain level as needed. Add salt, black pepper, chili powder, reserved beans and tasso (or chunk ham) and simmer boil for 2 hours. Serve over rice.

∾ ARLINGTON ∾

Arlington was built in the mid 1850's by Euphrazie Carlin, a wealthy planter and owner of many slaves. It is located East of Franklin in St. Martin Parish on La. 182. The Greek Revival mansion's facade features a pedimented portico, with wrought-iron balustrade and is supported by four wooden Corinthian Columns. The rear of the house, which is similar in design faces Bayou Teche. Arlington's interior is most attractive and has hallways allowing entrance from either side. It was beautifully restored in 1965 to its original plan by Senator and Mrs. Carl Bower.

CRAWFISH ETOUFFEE'

¼ LB	BUTTER
1 CUP	ONION, CHOPPED
½ CUP	BELL PEPPER, CHOPPED
¼ CUP	CELERY, FINELY CHOPPED
2 TBSP	GARLIC, MINCED
2 TBSP	PARSLEY FLAKES, DRIED
1 TSP	SALT
1 TSP	CAJUN SEASONING, SEE RECIPE PAGE 25
1 TBSP	ALL-PURPOSE FLOUR
1 CUP	CRAWFISH, CHICKEN STOCK OR WATER
1 LB PEELED	CRAWFISH TAILS

In a large skillet, melt butter on high heat. As soon as butter is almost melted, add onion, bell pepper, celery, garlic, parsley, salt, and Cajun seasoning. Stir well and simmer, lowering the heat slightly, until onion begin to wilt. Add flour and stir in well. Continue to stir until flour begins to stick to the bottom of the skillet. Slowly add stock a little at a time and stir until all is added and blended. Simmer for 2 minutes or until a bubble is reached. Add crawfish tails and stir well. Bring back to a bubble, reduce heat to low and simmer, covered, for 10 - 15 minutes. Serve over rice.

CRAWFISH PIE

THE PASTRY:

2 CUPS	ALL-PURPOSE FLOUR
1 TSP	SALT
⅔ CUP	SHORTENING
6-7 TBSP	COLD WATER

In a bowl, mix flour and salt. Add shortening a little at a time and blend cutting in with a fork or pastry tool (Note: you can do all this in a food processor). When all shortening is properly added the dough will form pea-sized balls. Add water and mix until dough is easy to form into a ball. Divide dough into 2 balls, one third for one and two thirds for the other. Roll out the larger ball and place into a pie pan. Roll out the other and set aside for the top.

THE FILLING

Preheat oven to 350°F. Prepare "Crawfish Etouffee" recipe page 40. Allow to cool to room temperature, fill prepared pie dough shell to ¼" from top and top with reserved dough. Reserve any remaining etouffee' for a topping to the pie. Cut slits into top shell, pinch the ends to seal, and place in oven for 30-35 minutes or until top is brown. Serve.

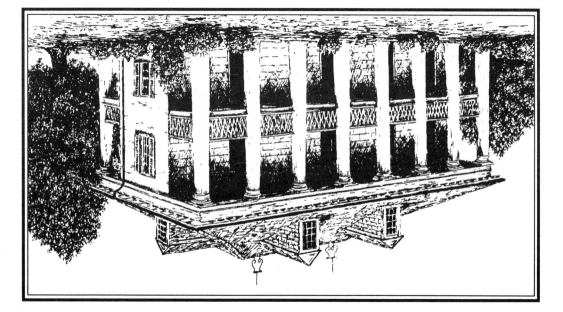

❧ BEAUREGARD HOUSE ❧

Located in Chalmette just below New Orleans. Beauregard House was built in the 1830's by James Gallier Sr. for the Marquis de Trava. It later became the home of Rene Beauregard, son of the famous Confederate General P.G.T. Beauregard. The house, only one room deep features large Doric columns on front and back. It is part of the Chalmette Historical Park and Cemetery complex, site of the 1812 Battle of New Orleans and is open to the public daily, at no charge.

⸜ Dirty Rice ⸝

The technique to follow will make it easy for you to store the meat mix for later use with freshly cooked rice. This will allow you to make plenty of the "meat base" and use it in a pinch to produce a great, quick main dish.

Meat Base:

1 lb	Ground Beef, 70% lean	2 tbsp	Garlic, finely minced
2 lb	Ground Pork Breakfast Type Sausage	2 tbsp	Parsley Flakes, dried
½ lb	Chicken Livers	2 tbsp	Whole Sweet Basil, dried
½ lb	Chicken Gizzards*	1 tsp	Salt
2 cups	Onion, finely chopped	1 tsp	Pepper, Black
1 cup	Bell Pepper, finely chopped	1 tsp	Cajun Seasoning,
½ cup	Celery, finely chopped		see recipe page 25

5-10 CUPS   COOKED RICE**   FRESH GREEN ONION, CHOPPED

*Cleaned of membrane and ground in a food processor. When gizzards are pulsed for 30 seconds add the chicken liver and pulse for an additional 30 seconds. Should be fine in texture.

** The amount of rice needed will depend on the desired texture of the finished product. Just add meat to rice or visa versa until it looks like you want.

In a large skillet, brown all meat, livers, and gizzards that have been prepared as directed above. When brown, drain off most of the oil, return to high heat and add remaining ingredients, except for the rice and green onion. Simmer for 15 minutes on medium to medium high heat, stir frequently, add a little water if sticking occurs. Mix with desired amount of hot rice, add green onion, mix well and allow to stand covered for 5 minutes. Serve. Remember to freeze the "meat base " mixture in quantities that will allow you to mix with freshly cooked rice for your future needs.

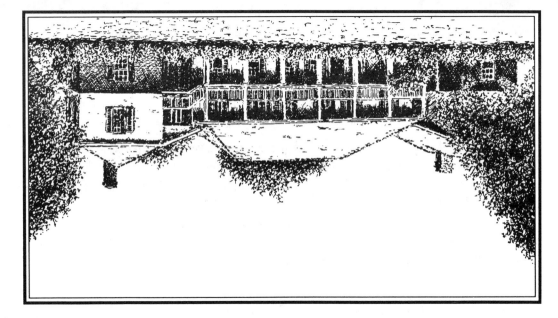

Ormond is located in Destrehan, along the River Road in St. Charles parish near New Orleans. Its central structure was built by Pierre Trepagnier toward the end of the Spanish regime. The two side wings, slightly taller, and uniquely joined to the main building, were added in 1811.

The house, one of the oldest in the Mississippi Delta, has been restored and somewhat modified in recent times. It presently is operated as a restaurant, house museum, and bed-and-breakfast inn.

ೞCHICKEN SAUCE PIQUANTE' ೞ

THIS IS A SPICY HOT DISH

2	WHOLE CHICKEN FRYERS	1 TSP	SALT
2 TBSP	OLIVE OIL	1 TSP	BLACK PEPPER
2 CUPS	ONION, CHOPPED	1 TSP	CAJUN SEASONING, SEE RECIPE PAGE 25
1 CUP	BELL PEPPER, CHOPPED	1 TSP	CAYENNE PEPPER
⅔ CUP	JALAPENO PEPPERS, FINELY CHOPPED IN PROCESSOR	6 OZ	TOMATO PASTE
		16 OZ	TOMATO SAUCE
½ CUP	CELERY, FINELY CHOPPED	1 CUP	RESERVED CHICKEN STOCK, PROVIDED IN RECIPE
2 TBSP	GARLIC, MINCED		
2 TBSP	PARSLEY FLAKES, DRIED	1	PREPARED ROUX RECIPE, SEE RECIPE PAGE 22
2 TBSP	WHOLE SWEET BASIL, DRIED		

Place chickens into a pot and cover with water by 2-3 inches. Bring to a boil, reduce heat to medium high and boil for 45 minutes. Remove chickens, reduce heat to low on stock. When chickens cool, pick all the meat and reserve. Place bones into boiling stock, bring water level to just above the bones and boil for 1 hour. Drain and allow stock to stand 20 minutes. Skim fat with ladle and reserve stock.

In a 4 quart pot, heat oil to hot. Add onion, bell pepper, jalapeno pepper, celery, garlic, parsley, basil, salt, red and black pepper, and Cajun seasoning. Stir until mixture begins to bubble. Add tomato paste and stir in well. Bring heat to high and continue to stir until paste begins to brown. Add tomato sauce and stir until completely blended. Add 1 cup reserved chicken stock and stir until blended. Bring to a boil, add roux and stir until blended. Reduce heat to lowest setting, cover and simmer for 1 hour, stirring occasionally. Return to high heat, add reserved chicken meat and stir well. Cover, reduce heat to low and simmer another 15 minutes, stirring only once. Serve over pasta or rice.

❧ RICHLAND ❧

Richland, located in East Feliciana Parish, forty miles northeast of Baton Rouge, was built in 1820 by Elias Norwood. The original house, built in the classic Green Revival style was not the typical Louisiana house of that period. It has been remodeled, first near the turn of the twentieth century and more recently by the late Charles Wilson, once president of General Motors and a former Secretary of Defense. Most of the changes made were to the interior of the house and with the exception of joining the once separate kitchen structure to the main house the exterior remains almost as it was when built.

⋙ STICKY CHICKEN ⋘

6	CHICKEN LEG AND THIGH QUARTERS	1 TSP	SALT
¼ LB	BUTTER OR MARGARINE	1 TSP	CAYENNE PEPPER
1 CUP	ONION, FINELY CHOPPED	3 TBSP	ALL-PURPOSE FLOUR
3 TBSP	GARLIC, MINCED	¼ CUP	WHITE WINE
1 TBSP	PARSLEY FLAKES	3 CUPS	CHICKEN STOCK

Wash leg and thigh quarters well. Place on a cutting board and remove the bone. Note: the butcher will do this for you if you desire for a small fee.

Melt 3 tbsp butter in a skillet on high heat. Place deboned chicken in the skillet skin side down. Set heat to medium high and fry the chicken until the bottom side is beginning to brown along the edges (about 10 minutes). Sprinkle with salt and pepper and turn. Cook 10 to 14 minutes or until chicken is done. It will stick, don't worry, just scrap the chicken out and set aside on a plate. DO NOT DRAIN ON PAPER! To the skillet add remaining butter and add onion, garlic and parsley and saute for 5 - 7 minutes. Add flour and stir in well. Continue to stir until flour is beginning to stick to the bottom of the pan. Return heat to highest setting and saute for 30 seconds. Add the wine and remove from heat immediately and stir until pan is clean of stuck residue. You are de-glazing the skillet.

Return to high heat. Add chicken stock stirring until all is blended. Adjust liquid for texture. Cover the skillet and simmer on low for 15 minutes. While the pot is simmering, remove the skin from the cooked chicken and discard. Cut the chicken into 1" pieces and return the chicken to the skillet and stir well. Continue to simmer for 3 minutes. Remove from heat and set aside covered for 10 minutes serve with rice or potatoes.

Evergreen is still the centerpiece of a working sugar plantation. It's two graceful curving stairways, large Doric columns, hipped roof topped with a large belvedere, together with symmetrical chimneys and dormer windows, create a beautiful structure almost epitomizing the typical Southern look.

The plantations slave cabins, pigeonnaires garconierres, carriage houses, and even the "Greek-revival" privy all remain—-making Evergreen one of the few "complete" plantations in south Louisiana. It is located on the west bank of the Mississippi, near Edgard, and is maintained as a private residence.

❧ LIVER AND ONIONS ❧

2 LB	FROZEN CALF LIVER,
	CLEANED, DEVEINED, AND SLICED
	SALT AND BLACK PEPPER TO TASTE
1 CUP	ALL-PURPOSE FLOUR
¼ LB	BUTTER
2 LARGE	ONIONS, CUT INTO ¼" RINGLETS
3 CUPS	CHICKEN OR PORK STOCK AT
	ROOM TEMPERATURE

Allow liver to thaw completely. Rinse liver well. Drain. In a large skillet, heat butter on medium heat. Sprinkle salt and pepper over the liver to taste, dredge in the flour. Raise heat to high and place floured liver carefully into the hot butter. Repeat until you have all the liver in the skillet. Reserve the flour.

Fry until brown. Turn only once and allow to brown on the other side. Remove and reserve. Add onion ringlets to skillet and cook until onions begin to brown. Remove and reserve keeping as much butter in the skillet as possible. Add more butter if you feel it is necessary. Add 2 tablespoons of the reserved flour and whisk until flour turns a dark brown, about the color of chocolate. Slowly add the stock, whisking as you add until all the stock is added and the mixture has blended into a thick sauce.

Return the liver and onions to the skillet and work liver into sauce. Reduce heat to low. Add liquid as needed. Simmer for 45 minutes on low heat or until the liver is tender. Serve over rice or with mashed potatoes, or if you are a little daring serve with your favorite pasta.

❦ TEZCUCO ❧

Tezcuco was built just before the Civil War for Benjamin Tureaud, and his bride, Aglae Bringer of the wealthy and influential Bringer family. It's style is called "Louisiana Cottage", though it's size matches many of it's more elaborate and grander counterparts. Magnificent, moss-draped oaks enhance the elaborate gardens and grounds.

The house, beautifully restored and furnished, is surrounded by a "village" of smaller structures of it's period, serving as accommodations, shops, a restaurant and service buildings for Tezcuco's "Bed-and-Breakfast" status.

It is located on the River Road one mile north of the Sunshine Bridge and is also open daily for tours for an entrance fee. Lunch and dinner is served in it's popular restaurant, which also features a charming Sunday brunch.

๑CHICKEN FRICASSEE' ๑

1	WHOLE CHICKEN FRYER
2 QUARTS	WATER
2 TBSP	BACON FAT OR HOG LARD
1 CUPS	ONION, CHOPPED
½ CUP	BELL PEPPER, CHOPPED
¼ CUP	CELERY, CHOPPED
2 TBSP	GARLIC, FINELY MINCED
1 TBSP	PARSLEY, DRIED
½ TBSP	WHOLE SAGE, DRIED
½ TBSP	SALT
½ TBSP	CAYENNE PEPPER
2 TBSP	WHITE WINE
¾ CUP	PREPARED ROUX, SEE RECIPE PAGE 22

In a 3 quart pot, boil chicken until completely cooked, about 45 minutes. Remove chicken and allow to cool. Strain and reserve stock. When chicken is cool, pick meat and reserve. Remove oil from stock and let stand at room temperature. Prepare all vegetables as directed.

In a large skillet, heat fat on high heat. Add onion, bell pepper, and celery and stir. Add garlic, parsley, sage, salt and cayenne pepper and stir well. Saute' for 5 minutes.

Next, add wine and stir in well. Add 3 cups reserved stock, stirring and blending constantly until all stock is added. Bring to a rapid boil, and add roux in small quantities and stir until desired stew-like texture is achieved. Stir well cover and simmer on medium low for 20 minutes. Add picked chicken and simmer another 15 minutes. Serve over cooked rice.

❧ GLENDALE ❧

Glendale, built in 1810, in the West Indies architectural style, epitomizes Louisiana's grand homes of that early 19th century period. It's two stories are topped by high and spacious attic. The house features a one-hundred-foot-wide front gallery and a raised basement. It is together built of stucco covered brick and hand-hewn timbers held together with wooden pegs. Though only a room-and-a-half deep, Glendale gives the appearance of a much larger structure.

With the exception of the octagonal tiles imported from Europe which cover the main level's floor, almost everything else in the house, both inside and out, was made from materials taken from the area. Glendale is a private home, located along the west side of the Mississippi, near Lucy, in St. John the Baptist Parish.

∞ Hogs Head Cheese ∞

3 LBS	PORK BUTT, CUBED	2 TBSP	WHOLE SWEET BASIL, DRIED
2 CUPS	ONION, CHOPPED	1 TSP	SALT
1 CUP	BELL PEPPER, CHOPPED	1 TSP	BLACK PEPPER
½ CUP	CELERY, FINELY CHOPPED	1 TSP	CAJUN SEASONING, SEE RECIPE PAGE 25
2 TBSP	GARLIC, MINCED	3 CUPS	WATER OR PORK STOCK
2 TBSP	PARSLEY FLAKES, DRIED	3 PKTS	UNFLAVORED GELATIN

In a 4 quart pot, brown all pork. Add all remaining ingredients, except for the gelatin. Bring mixture to a boil, cover and simmer on medium heat for 2 hours, stirring vigorously every 15 minutes. When completely cooked the meat should be shredded and completely reduced to a stringy consistency. Mix gelatin in 1 cup very hot water and add to the pork mixture and stir well. Place into a mold or glass casserole dish and chill until set. Remove from mold and serve with favorite crackers.

✷ CRAB BOIL ✷

KEEP LIVE CRABS ICED UP THE NIGHT BEFORE COOKING IF POSSIBLE. IF YOU DON'T HAVE THIS MUCH TIME, ICE UP AS LONG AS POSSIBLE. CRABS SHOULD NOT DIE FROM ICING THE NIGHT BEFORE.

18-20	QUARTS WATER	3 TBSP	CAYENNE PEPPER
2	MEDIUM ONIONS, QUARTERED	3 TBSP	BLACK PEPPER
5	INDIVIDUAL CLOVES GARLIC,	3	LEMONS QUARTERED
	PEELED NOT NECESSARY	24	LIVE CRABS, THE LAKE VARIETY
¼ CUP	LIQUID CRAB BOIL	¼ CUP	SALT

In a 28 quart (28 liter) pot filled to about ⅔ of capacity with water. Heat until a rolling boil. (Note: Use an outside boiler for best results but not necessary).

Next, add onion, garlic, crab boil, cayenne, black pepper, and lemons. Bring back to a boil, add crabs. Boil for 15 minutes. Remove from heat, add salt, stir, let stand for 5 minutes, drain and eat!

❧ St. Louis ❧

Located near Plaquemine, in Iberville Parish, St. Louis was named after the home state of its builder, Edward Gay, first president of the Louisiana Sugar Exchange.

The house, built in 1858, is an eclectic blend of architectural styles, featuring Greek Revival columns on both levels of its galleries combined with New Orleans style railings. A brick "cellar," unusual for Louisiana's marshy ground, is a feature seldom found in area plantation homes.

St. Louis is still in possession of members of the gay family, it was open to the public for a short time in the 1980's but is now privately maintained.

CRABMEAT AU GRATIN

¼ LB	BUTTER
1 CUP	ONION, MINCED
¼ CUP	GREEN ONION, MINCED
1 TBSP	GARLIC, MINCED
1 TBSP	SHALLOT, MINCED
¼ CUP	GREEN PEPPER, MINCED
¼ CUP	ALL-PURPOSE FLOUR
1½ CUP	WHIPPING CREAM
1 TSP	SALT
1 TSP	BLACK PEPPER OR ½ TSP CAYENNE
3	EGG YOLKS, WELL BEATEN
1 LB	LUMP CRABMEAT, CHECK CAREFULLY FOR SHELLS
1½ CUP	SHARP CHEDDAR CHEESE, SHREDDED COURSE

In a saucepan melt butter on medium heat. Add onions, green onion, garlic, shallot, bell pepper, and simmer 5 minutes. Add flour a little at a time, stirring until all mixed. Cook 5 more minutes stirring constantly. When flour begins to stick slightly, slowly add whipping cream and stir as you add all 1½ cups. Cook until mixture thickens, stirring consistently for about 4-5 minutes. Remove from heat. Stir in salt, pepper, egg yolks and stir until well blended. Fold in crab meat and ½ of the cheddar cheese until mixed well. (Try not to break up the crab too much).

Put in individually greased ramekin bowls and spread remaining cheese on top. Bake uncovered in a 350°F oven for 20 minutes or until cheese begins to brown. Serve.

❧ HOMEPLACE ❧

Built by the Fortier family in the early 1800's, Homeplace, also known as "The Keller House," or "Keller Homeplace," is located on the west bank of the Mississippi river, near Hahnville in St. Charles Parish.

Heirs of the Keller family still own this property which, though not open to the public, can be seen in many movies and television productions featuring stories occurring in the south Louisiana area.

Architecturally, the house is of early and typical French-Spanish design. It's interior rooms are asymmetrically sized, but all open to it's galleries which surround the entire stuccoed brick construction.

❧ SHRIMP IN A CAJUN BUCKET ❧

½ LB	JUMBO SHRIMP		2 CUPS	ONION, CHOPPED
½ LB	FETTUCCINI, UNCOOKED		1 CUP	CELERY, CHOPPED
½ CUP	LUMP CRAB MEAT		3 TBSP	GARLIC, MINCED
1 TBSP	CORN STARCH		¼ CUP	FRESH PARSLEY, CHOPPED
	VEGETABLE SPRAY		1 LB	VERY SMALL (GUMBO) SHRIMP, PEELED
2 CUPS	HEAVY CREAM		1 TBSP	ALL-PURPOSE FLOUR
¼ LB	BUTTER		½ CUP	FRESH GREEN ONION, CHOPPED

Peel jumbo shrimp (reserve peeling) leaving last rib with tail attached. Rinse small shrimp and reserve. Preheat oven to 350°F. Cook fettuccine. Carefully check lump crab meat for any shell and remove. To crab meat, add corn starch and 1 tbsp heavy cream and mix well. Place crab meat equally in two ½ cup ramekin bowls that have been sprayed with vegetable spray.

reserved shrimp shell into a 1 quart (liter) pot and add remaining heavy cream. Place on medium heat and stir well. As soon as cream begins to bubble, reduce heat to very low and stir frequently. While cream is heating up, in a large skillet, melt butter. Add onion, celery, and garlic, and saute' until onions begin to wilt. Add parsley and stir well. Add peeled jumbo shrimp and saute' until just cooked. Remove and reserve cooked jumbo shrimp. Add small (gumbo) shrimp to skillet and stir well. Saute' until shrimp are all pink. Add flour, and stir in well. Strain heavy cream into skillet and stir well. Bring to a rolling boil, reduce heat and stir well. Simmer 10 minutes, remove from heat. Add green onion and stir in well. Place pasta into bowl, place crab meat ramekin (removed from ramekin bowl) in center of pasta. Press the middle of crab meat gently until a pocket is formed, Arrange jumbo shrimp around crab meat, hanging tail into pasta. Spoon cream mixture around the ends of the shrimp and in the center of the bucket. Garnish with sprig of parsley and serve. Serves two.

❧ OAKLEY ❧

Oakley is a large two-story frame house built over a brick basement and is located above Baton Rouge near St. Francisville. It was built in 1808 on an 1770 Spanish land grant.

Its architectural design is rather simple, antedating the Greek Revival style used by plantation home builders in later years. Wooden louvered slats, its most unique feature, cover the upper gallery and part of the lower, allowing light and air while giving protection from the elements.

Oakley's most famous inhabitant was John James Audubon who painted thirty two of the birds in his masterwork, "The Birds Of America."

The 100 acre site is now part of the Louisiana park system, featuring nature trails and formal gardens. It is open daily to the public.

❧ Blackened Red Snapper ❧

I highly recommend that you do this outside because of the smoke from the high heat cooking. Be sure to have a burner outside that is capable of high temperature cooking.

1 tsp	Cayenne Pepper
1 tbsp	Whole Oregano
1 tbsp	Whole Thyme
1 tsp	Salt
1 tsp	Black Pepper
1	Red Snapper Filet, about 1lb.
	Cut into 1 inch wide steaks
9 tbsp	Butter
1 heavy	Skillet for Frying, preferably cast iron

Mix Cayenne pepper, oregano, thyme, salt, and black pepper together until totally blended. Place in a deep plate. As instructed, cut filets into 1 inch steaks cutting with the grain of the fish or top to bottom and not side to side. Wash fish well and dredge into the seasoning mixture.

Heat the skillet to very hot. Drop 2 tbsp of butter into pan and move around with spatula to melt quickly. Immediately lay coated fish steaks into the hot butter making sure that the fish gets into the butter evenly. Fry on high heat on each side for 1-2 minutes. Remove cooked fish add butter and continue until all is cooked (Do not drain). When all is cooked add remaining butter to pan, remove from heat and melt while stirring. Pour over cooked fish and serve.

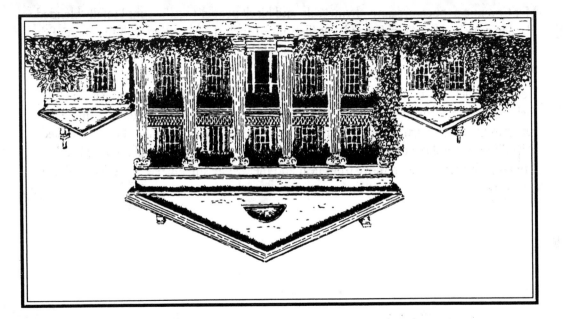

✑ MADEWOOD ✑

Located along Bayou Lafourche, near Napoleonville, Madewood is a magnificent white mansion built by Colonel Thomas Pugh, and designed by the noted architect Henry Howard.

Its construction, which took four years to complete, was begun in 1840. Sixty thousand slave-made bricks and hand-hewn timbers, all from the plantation grounds were used in its construction.

Madewood has been beautifully restored and furnished by the Marshall family of New Orleans in recent years. The house is open to the public for tours and for bed-and-breakfast overnight accommodations.

❧ Candied Yams ❧

5 LB	SWEET POTATO OR YAMS	1 TSP	NUTMEG, GROUND, OPTIONAL
1 CUP	DARK BROWN SUGAR	½ TSP	SALT
½ CUP	LIGHT BROWN SUGAR	3 TBSP	BUTTER
1 TBSP	CINNAMON, GROUND		

Boil sweet potatoes in water until tender at center. Reserve 2 cups of water. Allow to cool, peel, cut in half long ways and then across and set in a baking dish big enough to accommodate the potatoes (10x13 should do). Preheat oven to 350°F.

Sprinkle all sugar over top evenly, allowing some to fall in the cracks. Do the same with the cinnamon, nutmeg and salt. Place pieces of butter evenly spaced around the top of the boiled sweet potatoes. Pour 2 cups of the reserved potato water over the top, cover with foil and bake for 35 minutes. Uncover and bake for an additional 10 minutes. Serve.

∽ SMOTHERED OKRA ∽

3 LB	OKRA, RINSED WELL, DE-STEM, SLICED IN ½" SLICES	2 TBSP	GARLIC, MINCED
		2 TBSP	PARSLEY FLAKES, DRIED
3 TBSP	BACON, PORK FAT OR LARD	1 TSP	SALT
2 CUPS	ONION, CHOPPED	1 TSP	BLACK PEPPER
1 CUP	BELL PEPPER, CHOPPED	2 CUPS	TOMATO, SEEDED, DICED

Heat fat to hot, add onion, bell pepper, garlic, parsley, salt and pepper and simmer for 3 minutes. Add sliced okra and stir well. Cover and simmer for 10 minutes on medium low heat, stirring as needed. Add diced tomato and stir well. Cover, reduce heat to low and simmer an additional 20 minutes stirring as needed. Serve as vegetable or over rice.

Shadows-on-the-Teche, an 1831 "town-house" version of a Louisiana Greek Revival Plantation home is located on Main street in New Iberia, LA. It was built by David Weeks as his residence and the center of his plantation system.

The home's lush surroundings are reflected in its name. Magnificent, moss-draped oaks, flowering Magnolias, tall cypresses, crepe myrtles, jasmines, camellias, exotic ferns and other flora all cast long, lazy shadows.

The house was occupied by Federal troops during the Civil War as headquarters for General Banks. It remained in the family and was rescued from its deteriorating state by Weeks Hall who after restoring the house and gardens to its original glory gave the property to the National Trust for Historical Preservation who maintain and open the property to the public.

Chicken and Andouille Gumbo

3	WHOLE CHICKEN FRYERS	2 TBSP	PARSLEY FLAKES, DRIED
4 QTS	RESERVED STOCK, PROVIDED IN RECIPE	1 TBSP	SALT
		1 TBSP	BLACK PEPPER
4	PORTIONS PREPARED ROUX, SEE RECIPE PAGE 22	1 TBSP	CAJUN SEASONING, SEE RECIPE PAGE 25
		2 LBS	ANDOUILLE, SLICED ¼" THICK
2 CUPS	ONION, CHOPPED	1 CUP	GREEN ONION, CHOPPED
1 CUP	BELL PEPPER, CHOPPED		FILE' OPTIONAL AND ADDED ONLY AT THE TABLE, NOT TO THE POT
½ CUP	CELERY, FINELY CHOPPED		
2 TBSP	GARLIC, MINCED		

Boil chickens until falling apart (about 45 minutes). Return stock along with enough water to make 6 quarts to the pot and bring to a boil. Meanwhile, cool chicken and pick off all the meat, reserve meat. Return bones to stock and boil an additional hour. Remove bones and strain stock of all but liquid. Allow to stand for 30 minutes, remove all oil from top of stock, and return 4 quarts to a clean 8 quart pot.

Bring stock to a boil and add roux until added and blended. Add onion, bell pepper, celery, garlic, parsley, salt, pepper and Cajun Seasoning and stir well. Bring to a boil and simmer on medium high heat for 30 minutes. Add andouille and bring back to a bubble. Simmer an additional 20 minutes. Add reserved, picked chicken meat to pot and stir well. Cover and simmer on low, undisturbed for 10 minutes. Remove from heat and serve over rice like a soup. Top with green onion, and/or file' if desired.

⌒ ROSEDOWN ⌒

The center section of Rosedown, built of cypress and painted white, was built in 1834 by Daniel Turnbull, a descendent of George Washington. Two stuccoed, brick, Greek Revival wings were added in 1840.

Elegant furnishings, many original to the house, and a magnificent formal garden and alley of Live Oaks, make Rosedown one of the most visited attractions in Louisiana.

Members of the Turnbull family occupied the property until 1956. It was then acquired by Mr. & Mrs. Milton Underwood of Houston, Texas who restored the house and gardens opening it to the public several years later.

Rosedown is located on LA. 10 just east of St. Francisville.

❧Shrimp Bisque ❧

1 LB	VERY LARGE SHRIMP, PEELED, DEVEINED, BUTTERFLIED, RESERVE PEELING	2 TBSP	PARSLEY FLAKES, DRIED
		2 TBSP	WHOLE SWEET BASIL, DRIED
4 CUPS	HEAVY CREAM	1 TSP	SALT
1 CUP	WATER	1 TSP	TURMERIC
¼ LB	BUTTER	2 TSP	WHOLE THYME
2 CUPS	ONION, CHOPPED	1 TSP	BLACK PEPPER
1 CUP	BELL PEPPER, CHOPPED	1 TSP	CAJUN SEASONING, SEE RECIPE PAGE 25
½ CUP	CELERY, CHOPPED FINE	¼ CUP	ALL-PURPOSE FLOUR
2 TBSP	GARLIC, MINCED	1 CUP	GREEN ONION, CHOPPED

Place reserved shrimp peeling into 4 cups of heavy cream and 1 cup of water. Bring to a boil on high heat, reduce to a low bubble and simmer for 20 minutes. Strain and reserve 4 cups of cream stock. Add water to make 4 cups if necessary.

In a large skillet, melt butter on high heat. As soon as butter is almost melted, add onion, bell pepper, celery, garlic, parsley, basil, salt, turmeric, whole thyme, black pepper and Cajun seasoning. Stir well and simmer, lowering the heat slightly, until onion begin to wilt.

Add flour and stir in well. Continue to stir until flour begins to stick to the bottom of the skillet. Slowly add stock a little at a time and stir until all is added and blended. Simmer for 2 minutes or until a bubble is reached. Add shrimp and stir well. Bring back to a bubble, reduce heat to low and simmer, covered, for 25 - 30 minutes. Serve in a soup bowl topped with fresh green onion.

◈ ASPHODEL ◈

Asphodel is located in East Feliciana Parish on La. 68 approximately 25 miles from Baton Rouge. The smallish Greek Revival house was built by Benjamin Kendrich in 1833. Six white Doric columns support a gabled roof which features two dormer windows. Small, similar appearing wings are used for overnight accommodations, include a cabin originally built in 1850.

Several Hollywood movies were photographed here, the most notable "The Long Hot Summer", which starred Paul Newman, Joanne Woodward and Orson Welles.

✀ GRILLADES ✀

GRILLADES ARE THINLY SLICED PORK, EITHER RAW OR ALREADY COOKED, THAT IS FRIED IN PORK FAT, OR BACON FAT, AND SERVED WITH RICE OR POTATOES. THE SEASONING IS THE SIGNATURE OF THE DISH. I WILL SHARE ONE WAY, BUT BE CREATIVE.

1 4-5 LB	BOSTON BUTT OR SHANK PORK ROAST
½ CUP	WORCESTERSHIRE SAUCE
½ CUP	SOY SAUCE
¼ CUP	GARLIC, MINCED
1 CUP	RED ONION, MINCED
½ CUP	ITALIAN DRESSING
1 TSP	CAJUN SEASONING, SEE RECIPE PAGE 25
1 TSP	SALT
3 TBSP	BACON FAT OR PORK FAT

Clean pork roast of all external fat and any large runs of internal fat if possible. Slice the pork against the grain very thin (about ⅛-inch thick) and try to cut so that the diameter of the piece of meat is as large as possible.

Mix all remaining ingredients. Dip slices of pork into the marinade mixture and place in a sealable container. Pour remaining marinade over the pork slices, seal and place in refrigerator for at least 2 hours, overnight is better.

In a skillet, melt fat to hot and add pork to oil. Fry until brown. Continue process until all is added. Serve with rice or potatoes. Optional Note: If you remove the fat from the skillet, bring to high heat, add a little flour, brown and then slowly add some stock or water to the pan, stirring constantly until blended and the bottom of the pan is clean, you will make a great sauce for the grillades.

❦ CHRETIEN POINT ❧

Chretien Point was built by Hypolite Chretien II in the early 1830's on a 1776 Spanish land grant purchased in 1799 by his father. Six two-storied Tuscan pillars support a front gallery and eaves of the hipped roof. Inside, Chretien is beautifully preserved and furnished.

During the Civil War, a battle was fought on the plantation grounds. A story is told that Hypolite Chretien II, though sick and feeble, saved the house from destruction by Federal forces, by giving a secret Masonic sign that was honored by Federal General Banks, a fellow Mason. Though the house was spared, the rest of the plantation buildings were destroyed.

Chretien Point is located 8 miles south of Opelousas in St. Landry Parish.

Crawfish Fettuccine

1/4 LB	BUTTER		2 TBSP	ALL-PURPOSE FLOUR
1 CUPS	ONION, CHOPPED		2½ CUPS	HEAVY CREAM
½ CUP	CELERY, FINELY CHOPPED		½ CUP	SHARP CHEDDAR CHEESE, SHREDDED
2 TBSP	GARLIC, MINCED			
2 TBSP	PARSLEY FLAKES, DRIED		1 LB	CRAWFISH TAILS
2 TBSP	WHOLE SWEET BASIL, DRIED			COOKED FETTUCCINE
½ TSP	SALT			PARMESAN CHEESE
1 TSP	CAJUN SEASONING, SEE RECIPE PAGE 25			GREEN ONION, CHOPPED

Heat butter to hot, add onion celery, garlic, parsley, basil, salt and Cajun seasoning. Saute' for 5 minutes. Add flour and stir in well. Stir until flour just begins to brown. Add heavy cream a little at a time, stirring and blending until all is added and blended. Mixture should be slightly thick. Sprinkle cheese over top of mixture. Cover, reduce heat to low and simmer for 10 minutes, stirring twice. Add crawfish tails and stir in well. Cover, and simmer on low for another 15 minutes stirring twice. Keep covered, remove from heat and allow to stand for 5 minutes. Serve over cooked fettuccine, topped with parmesan cheese and green onion.

St. Joseph, located near Vacherie in St. James parish was built in 1820 by Dr. Cazamine Mericq, a native of France. Most historians state that the house was sold to Louisiana's most wealthy and most notable planter, Valcour Aime as a wedding present for one of his daughters in 1847.

After the Civil War the plantation was acquired by Joseph Waguespack. The two-storied, hipped-roof, brick structure West Indies styled structure is still maintained by descendants of Mr. Waguespack.

STUFFED CRABS

1 LB	LUMP CRAB MEAT, PICKED CLEAN OF SHELL	½ TBSP	WHOLE SWEET BASIL, DRIED
¼ LB	BUTTER	½ TBSP	WHOLE THYME, DRIED
½ CUPS	ONION, MINCED	¼ TSP	SALT
¼ CUP	BELL PEPPER, MINCED	¼ TSP	CAJUN SEASONING, SEE RECIPE PAGE 25
1 TBSP	CELERY, FINELY MINCED	½ CUP	SEAFOOD STOCK OR WATER
½ TBSP	GARLIC, MINCED	1 TBSP	LEMON JUICE
½ TBSP	PARSLEY FLAKES, DRIED	2 CUPS	SEASONED BREAD CRUMBS

In a large skillet, heat butter to melted. Add onion, bell pepper, celery, garlic, parsley, basil, whole thyme, salt and Cajun seasoning. Simmer until onion begins to wilt. Add ½ cup reserved seafood stock and lemon juice and bring to a low bubble. Add crab meat and stir in well, (don't worry about the meat breaking up, the texture will be good for the stuffing). Cover mixture, reduce heat to lowest setting and allow to simmer undisturbed for 5 minutes. Remove from heat, do not uncover and allow to stand for another 5 minutes. Uncover, and add bread crumbs until mixture can be handled. Allow to cool to room temperature.

Preheat oven to 350°F. Pat cooled mixture into balls, roll into seasoned bread crumbs and place on foiled crab shaped shell. Place in oven and bake for 25 minutes or until brown. Serve.

BAYSIDE

Bayside, a two-story house of brick and bousillage, is located west of Jeannerette along Bayou Teche in Iberia Parish. Built by Francis D.Richardson in 1859, it features six massive Doric Columns supporting wooden balustered galleries on its front and rear. Interior appointments include cypress floors, richly paneled doors and marble mantles.

Mr. Richardson was a classmate and friend of Edgar Allen Poe. He also served in the Louisiana Legislature before the Civil War.

∼ CORNBREAD DRESSING ∼

THE CORNBREAD:

4 CUPS	CORNMEAL, YELLOW		1 TBSP	SUGAR
1 CUP	SELF-RISING FLOUR		1 TBSP	BAKING POWDER
4	EGGS		½ CUP	MILK, BUTTERMILK OR
1 TSP	SALT			EVAPORATED MILK

Mix all ingredients until completely blended. Put into a greased pan and bake at 400°F for 35-45 minutes. Remove, cool, and crumble into a large mixing bowl. Reserve.

THE MIX:

1 LB	GROUND BEEF, 70% LEAN		2 TBSP	PARSLEY FLAKES, DRIED
2 LBS	GROUND PORK BREAKFAST TYPE SAUSAGE		2 TBSP	WHOLE SWEET BASIL, DRIED
½ LB	CHICKEN LIVERS, MINCED		1 TSP	SALT

2 CUPS	ONION, CHOPPED	1 TSP	BLACK PEPPER
1 CUP	BELL PEPPER, CHOPPED	1 TSP	CAJUN SEASONING, SEE RECIPE PAGE 25
½ CUP	CELERY, CHOPPED	2 CUPS	CHICKEN STOCK
2 TBSP	GARLIC, MINCED	2 CUPS	CREAM OF CHICKEN SOUP

In a large skillet, brown all meat, and chicken livers. When brown, drain off most of the oil, return to high heat and add remaining ingredients, except stock and soup. Stir well. Add stock and cream of chicken soup, stir well. Simmer for 15 minutes on medium to medium high heat, stir frequently. Remove from heat.

THE ASSEMBLY:

| 2 CUPS | MILK | 6 | EGGS |

Preheat oven to 350°F. Mix cornbread, meat mix, milk and eggs together in a large bowl. Pour into a large greased baking pan, cover with foil and bake for 30 minutes. Raise heat to 450°F, uncover and bake another 10 minutes. Serve.

❧ HOUMAS HOUSE ❧

One of the best known Louisiana plantation homes, Houmas House was built by Col. John Preston in 1850 in front of and connected at it's upper level to an earlier (1780) and smaller house.

The property was purchased by John Burnside in 1857 who expanded it's acreage to more than 2,000 acres of sugar producing crops. He operated the plantation until his death in 1881.

In 1940, the house, which had deteriorated considerably, was acquired by Dr. George Crozat, a New Orleans dentist. He restored the house and gardens to it's original magnificence. Members of the Crozat family still own and operate Houmas House. It's architecture and setting epitomizes what most think of as a true antebellum southern plantation.

✿ Oyster Dressing ✿

1 QUART	OYSTERS, CLEANED, LIQUEUR STRAINED AND RESERVED
2 TBSP	OLIVE OIL
1 CUPS	ONION, CHOPPED
2 TBSP	SHALLOT, MINCED
½ CUP	GREEN ONION, MINCED
1 TBSP	GARLIC, MINCED
1 TBSP	PARSLEY FLAKES, DRIED
1 TSP	WHOLE THYME
1 TSP	SALT
1 TSP	BLACK PEPPER
1¼ CUP	SEASONED BREAD CRUMBS

Place ½ of cleaned oysters into a blender along with ⅔ cup of the liqueur. Blend until oysters are liquefied. Reserve with whole oysters.

In a large skillet, heat oil to hot, add onion, shallot, green onion, garlic, parsley, thyme, salt and black pepper. Stir well, cover and simmer on medium heat for 10 minutes. Add liquefied oysters to skillet and stir well. Bring to a bubble. Cover and simmer on low for 10 minutes. Add whole oysters and stir well. Bring to a bubble, cover, reduce heat to lowest setting and let simmer undisturbed for 4 minutes. Remove from heat and allow to stand covered for an additional 5 minutes. Uncover, and add 1 cup bread crumbs until completely blended.

Preheat oven to 350°F. Place oyster mixture in an ample casserole dish, sprinkle remaining bread crumbs over top. Cover and bake for 25 minutes. Uncover, raise heat to 400°F and bake for 10 minutes. Serve.

❧ OAK ALLEY ❧

A magnificent alley of twenty eight oak trees approximately three hundred years old dominates the setting of this Greek Revival mansion originally called Beau Sejour. It was built in 1836 by Jaques Roman, brother of the Louisiana governor along the river in Vacherie.

The house was designed by architect George Swainey. It features twenty eight huge columns and at one time had twenty eight slave cabins, numbers which matched the dominant oaks.

Oak Alley was acquired by Mr. and Mrs. Andrew Stewart in 1925. They began an "adaptive" renovation, moved in, and opened the house to the public.

It is still maintained as a house museum and in addition to tours of the house and grounds, offers overnight accommodations, and a restaurant. It is one of Louisiana's most notable and popular tourist attractions.

❧ PORK JAMBALAYA ❧

3 LB	PORK BUTT OR LOIN	3 TBSP	WHOLE SWEET BASIL
½ CUP	PREPARED ROUX,	1 TBSP	SALT
	RECIPE ON PAGE 22	1 TSP	CAYENNE PEPPER
¼ LB	BUTTER	1 TSP	BLACK PEPPER
2 CUPS	ONION, CHOPPED	2 QTS	CHICKEN OR PORK STOCK OR WATER
1 CUP	BELL PEPPER, CHOPPED	4 CUPS	LONG GRAIN OR CONVERTED
½ CUP	CELERY, CHOPPED		WHITE RICE
3 TBSP	GARLIC, MINCED	1 CUP	GREEN ONION, CHOPPED
3 TBSP	PARSLEY FLAKES		

Trim pork of bones & external fat. Cut pork into 1" cubes, cover and reserve until needed.

Next, in a 6 quart pot, heat butter on high heat until melted. Add onion, bell pepper, celery, garlic, parsley, basil, salt and pepper and stir well. Continue to simmer on high until onion begins to wilt. Add pork and stir well. Continue to stir until pork is a nice brown color.

Add stock (or water) and stir well. Bring to a rapid boil and add reserved roux. Stir until roux is completely blended. Bring back to a rolling boil.

Reduce heat to maintain a low boil and cook until pork is 85% cooked.

Add uncooked rice and stir well. Bring back to a boil and stir again. Cover and reduce heat to lowest setting. Simmer for 10 minutes. Uncover and stir well. Cover and simmer for another 10 minutes. Uncover, stir, remove from heat. Cover and allow to stand for 5 minutes. Stir in green onion and serve. Serves 10 - 15.

✑ SAN FRANCISCO ✑

Built in a style best described as "Steamboat gothic," San Francisco is located on the River Road, just near Reserve, LA. It was built in the 1850's by Edmund Marmillon and his son Antoine.

The house, restored in recent years, is elaborately furnished and features a melange' of accouterments: stained glass windows, gilded moldings, hand-painted ceilings, faux-marble and lapus lazuli mantels, and copper-domed cisterns on each side. Much of the formal gardens in front of the house has been lost due to the encroachment of the Mississippi River.

San Francisco, one of the most visited sites in South Louisiana, is open daily for tours.

☙ Boiled Shrimp ☜

5 LB	LARGE SHRIMP, HEADS ON IF POSSIBLE, 21-25 PER POUND OR LARGER	1 PKG	CRAB AND SHRIMP BOIL
		2 TBSP	LIQUID CRAB BOIL
		2 TBSP	CAYENNE PEPPER
3 GAL	WATER	¼ CUP	SALT

I highly recommend that you do this outside if possible on a single jet or high capacity burner that can safely support a full large pot.

In a 5 gallon (20 quart) pot, equipped with basket if possible, heat water to a rolling boil. Add packaged and liquid crab boil, cayenne pepper and salt and stir well. Be careful not to break the seasoning bag. Bring back to a rolling boil and add all shrimp at the same time. Gently stir, bring back to a boil and boil for 6 minutes. Cover the pot, remove from heat and allow to stand undisturbed for an additional 5 minutes. Drain and serve, hot or cold.

༄ Chicken Roulades ༄

2	CHICKEN LEG AND THIGH QUARTER, DE-BONED
½ CUP	CORNBREAD DRESSING, SEE RECIPE PAGE 106
	PINCH OF SALT AND PEPPER
	PAN SPRAY
1 CUP	WATER

Place de-boned leg and thigh quarter on board, skin side down. Place about ½ cup of uncooked cornbread dressing in the center of the chicken. Be sure to shape along the entire center from end to end. Gently roll the chicken over the dressing and continue to roll until the seam is at the bottom of the chicken.

Place in a pan sprayed with pan spray. Pour in water, cover and bake for 45 minutes in a 350°F oven. Uncover, return to oven, raise heat to 400°F, bake until brown (about 15 minutes). Serves 2.

Nottoway, the largest of the existing Louisiana plantation homes, was built in 1841 by John Hampton Randolph. It was designed by the noted New Orleans architect, Henry Howard in the Italiante style, somewhat different from the Greek Revival styled mansion popular at the time.

The house has *65 rooms and almost 65,000 square feet.* A large, first level ballroom, finished completely in white is the focal point of the house. The beautiful room served its purpose well as seven of Mr. Randolph's eight daughters were married here.

Nottoway was restored in recent years and it continues to operate as a house museum with bread-and-breakfast accommodations. It also offers catering services for almost any event.

❧ SYRUP CAKE ❧

¼ LB	BUTTER, SOFTENED	1 TSP	SALT
½ CUP	SUGAR	½ TSP	BAKING SODA
2 CUPS	PURE CANE SYRUP	½ CUP	BUTTERMILK
2	EGGS	2 TSP	VANILLA
2 CUPS	ALL-PURPOSE FLOUR		

Combine butter and sugar together until blended. Add syrup and blend completely. Add flour, salt and baking soda, alternating with buttermilk and vanilla, and mix until completely combined and blended well.

Preheat oven to 350°F. Oil and flour a bundt type pan. Pour cake mixture into pan. Place into oven and bake for about 45 minutes or until toothpick comes out clean at the deepest part of the pan.

❧ RICE PUDDING ❧

3 CUPS	MILK	¾ CUP	SUGAR
1½ CUPS	COOKED RICE	1 TSP	VANILLA
1½ TBSP	BUTTER, MELTED	½ TSP	SALT
3	LARGE EGGS, BEATEN	1 CUP	PECANS, CHOPPED

In a 1½ quart pot heat to hot (just before boiling) the milk. Add rice and butter and blend in well, remove from heat. In a separate bowl, combine sugar, vanilla, salt pecans and eggs. Add rice and milk mixture to egg mixture a little at a time and mix until all is combined. Grease a 9-inch square pan and pour mixture into pan. Pour ½ inch water in a 10x10 inch pan and place rice mixture pan into it. Bake at 350°F for 1 hour until firm. Serves 4-6.

Reportedly built by a wayward member of the Lloyd's of London family, this beautiful house, an eclectic blend of several architectural styles, stands along bayou Boeuf, near Meeker, in Rapides Parish.

It has been restored in recent years by the Fitzgerald family who open the house to the public for tours.

Interestingly, Loyd's Hall is one of those antebellum mansions that abound with ghosts. Two such apparitions appear on a regular basis, one that of a Yankee soldier who was badly injured during the Civil War and who died in one of the slave cabins and the other that of a Confederate soldier who was hanged on the plantation grounds. Supposedly both ghosts are "friendly" and not "scary" when they appear.

ॐ Custard Tart – Tart ta la Bouille' ॐ

THE CUSTARD:

2	EGGS	2½ CUPS	MILK
3 TBSP	FLOUR	2 TSP	VANILLA
½ CUP	SUGAR		

Beat eggs well. Add sugar and blend well. Add flour and blend well. Set aside. Next, heat milk until a boil just begins. Remove form heat and add a little of the hot milk to the egg mixture, whisking as you add about 1/4th of the milk. Return milk to heat, add egg mixture to the milk and whisk on high heat until mixture begins to thicken. Add vanilla. Remove from heat and whisk for 2 minutes. Add to prepared pie dough.

THE PASTRY:

1½ CUPS	ALL-PURPOSE FLOUR	1 TSP	SALT
¼ CUP	SUGAR	½ CUP	SHORTENING
¼ TSP	BAKING POWDER	5-6 TBSP	COLD WATER

In a bowl, mix flour sugar, baking powder and salt. Add shortening a little at a time and blend cutting in with a fork or pastry tool (Note: you can do all this in a food processor). When all shortening is properly added the dough will form pea-sized balls. Add water and mix until dough is easy to form into a ball. Roll out the dough ball and place into a pie pan. Pinch the edges to scallop. I like it better without a top crust. Set aside.

Preheat the oven to 400°F. Place egg and milk mixture to pie crust and bake for 30-35 minutes. Set on cooling rack to room temperature. Serve best refrigerated.

✑ OAKLAWN MANOR ✑

Oaklawn Manor, a magnificent Greek Revival mansion is located along Bayou Tech near Franklin. Entrance to the plantation is through a long winding drive that ambles through one of the largest grove of live oaks in the country.

The house, originally built in 1837, was rebuilt in 1926 after a fire destroyed its interior. Materials from New Orleans and all over the world created an extravagant restructure.

The latest owners have added even more furnishings to the 15,000 square-foot mansion. A collection of Audubons, Selbys and Don Govez wood carvings are splendidly displayed.

Oaklawn Manor is open for tours daily.

⊸ BEIGNETS ⊶

3-3½ CUPS	ALL-PURPOSE FLOUR
2 TBSP	BUTTER FLAVORED SHORTENING
¼ CUP	SUGAR
½ TSP	SALT
½ CUP	EVAPORATED MILK
1	EGG, SLIGHTLY BEATEN
1 PKG	DRY YEAST
¾ CUP	WARM WATER (115 TO 125°F)
3 CUPS	PEANUT OIL FOR FRYING
	CONFECTIONERS SUGAR

In a bowl mix 2 cups flour with shortening and whisk until completely blended together. Add sugar and salt and blend. Mix yeast with warm water until yeast is totally dissolved. Let stand for 2 minute. Add to flour mixture along with evaporated milk and egg and mix well. Slowly add flour until a soft dough is formed. Turn out dough on a floured surface and work until satin texture (do not overwork). Roll out to about 1/8" thickness and cut into 2" squares. Fry in hot oil (360°F to 375°F) until brown on one side. Flip over and brown other side. Place on paper towels, dust with confectioners sugar and serve. Makes 25 to 30 beignets.

☙ BOCAGE ❧

Bocage is located on the River Road two miles North of Burnside in Ascension Parish. It was built as a wedding gift from Marius Bringier, a prominent Louisiana planter, for his daughter Francoise and her husband Cristophe Colomb, a descendant of America's discoverer.

The home is a rectangular, two-story building of wood above and brick below. Its front gallery and entablatured roof is supported by six large square pillars, and a pair of slimmer pillars at the center.

In recent years, Bocage has been beautifully restored and maintained by members of the Crozat and Kohlsdorf families.

❧ BREAD PUDDING ❧

1	30" LOAF FRESH FRENCH BREAD	2 CUPS	GRANULATED SUGAR
3	EGGS, SLIGHTLY BEATEN	2 TBSP	VANILLA EXTRACT
2 CUPS	WHOLE MILK	¼ CUP	BUTTER
2 CUPS	HEAVY CREAM OR EVAPORATED MILK		

Break up bread into small pieces. Put into large mixing bowl. In a bowl mix eggs, milk, heavy cream, sugar, and vanilla extract. Pour mixture over bread. Mix with your hands squeezing bread and pushing down into milk mixture until bread is saturated. Allow to stand for 10 minutes. Meanwhile melt butter and pour into a pan large enough to hold the entire mixture to ½ full. Pre-heat oven to 350°F. Pour mixture into greased pan and even out from end to end and side to side. Bake for 45 minutes or until completely brown on top (note: if ends are browning too fast and middle is not cooking as fast, then lower temperature and extend cooking time until total top is browned). Serves 10.

∾ New Orleans Butter Rum Sauce ∾

¼ LB	BUTTER	3	EGG YOLKS, SLIGHTLY BEATEN
½ CUP	CONFECTIONERS SUGAR	3 TBSP	DARK RUM
¼ CUP	LIGHT BROWN SUGAR		
¼ CUP	PURE CANE SYRUP OR OTHER SUGAR SYRUP		

Note: this must be done in a double boiler type situation. If you don't have a double boiler, then a metal bowl over boiling water will suffice. Be careful of steam burning your skin.

In a double-boiler melt butter and add all sugar and whisk until blended. Continue to whisk until sugar dissolves into butter and is very hot. Add syrup and whisk in well. Slowly add the egg yolks whisking constantly until blended. Remove from heat and continue to whisk until mixture begins to cool. Add rum and whisk until completely blended. Serve over bread pudding, cake or ice cream.

☙ NEW ORLEANS PECAN PRALINES ❧

¼ LB	BUTTER	½ CUP	EVAPORATED MILK
1½ CUPS	GRANULATED SUGAR	1 TSP	VANILLA EXTRACT
¾ CUPS	LIGHT BROWN SUGAR	½ CUP	PECAN PIECES
½ CUP	BUTTERMILK		

Melt butter on high heat. Add all sugar and blend completely with wire whisk or large spoon. As soon as mixture begins to liquefy and bubble, add buttermilk and evaporated milk and whisk until totally blended (Keep on high heat and continue to whisk and do not stop until you remove from heat). Boil until mixture reaches the soft ball stage (use a candy thermometer until you recognize the texture or just drop a ball of candy into cold water and check for soft ball stage. Remove from heat and add vanilla and stir in well whipping with whisk or spoon. Next quickly add pecan pieces and whip in well. Spoon out onto prepared waxed paper into desired sized pralines. Allow to cool completely before you eat.

∼ BANANAS FOSTER ∼

¼ CUP	BUTTER	4-5	BANANAS, PEELED
¼ CUP	LIGHT BROWN SUGAR	3 TBSP	DARK RUM
½ TSP	GROUND CINNAMON	1 TBSP	ORANGE JUICE
½ TSP	GROUND NUTMEG	1 TSP	LEMON JUICE
3 TBSP	BANANA LIQUEUR	4 SCOOPS	VANILLA ICE CREAM

Slice bananas long ways then cut across 3 times giving you 8 pieces per banana, reserve. In a 10" skillet, heat butter on high heat. Add brown sugar, cinnamon and nutmeg and whisk together with butter. Add banana liqueur and whisk in well. Add bananas and allow to come to a bubble. Continue to saute' for 5 minutes. Next, add rum, bring to a rapid bubble (you should pay close attention not to evaporate liquid.) As soon as liquid is very hot, ignite by spilling just a small amount into the fire or use a long lighter. Swirl liquid in pan to maintain fire until fire is out. Add orange and lemon juice and swirl to blend. Spoon over ice cream and serve immediately.

✺ METRIC CONVERSION CHART ✺

Distance measurement will only be in inches since we will be finding out how big a pan to use so all you have to know is: 1 inch or 1" equals 2.5cm or centimeters

TEMPERATURE CONVERSIONS

AMERICAN	METRIC*	AMERICAN	METRIC*	AMERICAN	METRIC*
100°F	38°C	250°F	122°C	375°F	190°C
150°F	66°C	300°F	149°C	400°F	205°C
200°F	94°C	325°F	165°C	450°F	235°C
		350°F	175°C		

Dry measurement consists of mainly weight otherwise measurements will be by volume. Note here that the term "ounce" as it is used here refers to a measure of weight.

MEASURE	EQUIVALENT	METRIC*	MEASURE	EQUIVALENT	METRIC*
¼ lb	4 ounces	113g	2.2 lb	35.2 ounces	1 kg
½ lb	8 ounces	225g	1 ounce	—	28g
1 lb	16 ounces	450g			

Volume measurement will be the most frequently used conversion. This will help you to make a close conversion for successful cooking. Note that the term "ounce" applies here to liquid ounce.

MEASURE	EQUIVALENT	METRIC*	MEASURE	EQUIVALENT	METRIC*
1 teaspoon	—	5 ml	½ cup	8 tablespoons	125ml
1 tablespoon	3 teaspoons	15ml	1 cup	16 tablespoons	250ml
2 tablespoons	1 ounce	30ml	1 pint	2 cups	500ml
¼ cup	4 tablespoons	60ml	1 quart	4 cups	1 liter
⅓ cup	5 tbsp. + 1 tsp	80ml			

*Note: Metric conversions are rounded off to make conversion easier. Exact conversion is not practical and should not effect recipe performance in this book.

∽ Louisiana Products ∾

Wherever I go to demonstrate cooking I am constantly asked for information about ordering Louisiana products once the out of state (or country) buyer gets home. It also occurred to me that many people are receiving this book as a gift or are buying without meeting someone who can give information about Louisiana products to them. If you write to me and provide your mailing address, I will be happy to provide you with Louisiana businesses that carry meats, spices and gifts. The offering is adequate to provide you with sources of quality hard to get products out of our fair state.

If you have received this book as a gift, have ordered from me directly or you purchased this book out of Louisiana, and are having trouble getting the information that you want, then don't hesitate to write to me:

Remy Laterrade
P.O. Box 3942
Lafayette, LA 70502-3942

If you haven't had a chance to visit Louisiana, then I invite you to enjoy our "food, folks and fun" as well as the finest place in the country for architecture and other great sights. The plantations, the theme parks, the music, food and culture are all here for you to come and enjoy. While you are making your plans to visit us, then please consider visiting Lafayette. We are located on I-10 exit #'s 100, 101 and 103.

YA'LL COME!

ORDER MORE BOOKS NOW!!!

I have more cookbooks in stock now! If you are having problems getting extra copies of "'DAT LITTLE LOUISIANA PLANTATION COOKBOOK", "'DAT LITTLE NEW ORLEANS CREOLE COOKBOOK", "'DAT LITTLE CAJUN COOKBOOK", or you want to get a copy of my first cookbook, "I WANT 'DAT CAJUN COOKBOOK", then use the order form following this page to order more books.

If you are interested in getting on my mailing list, then just drop me a letter requesting it, as outlined in the "LOUISIANA SECTION" on pages 141 and 142.

Ordering is easy…just fill our your name and "UPS" shipping address as well as your "mailing" address. Please give your phone number should there be any problems. Fill out how many books you want and add prices according to instructions. Be sure to add shipping and handling as directed.

Mail to the address given, allow 4-6 weeks for delivery.

'DAT LITTLE LOUISIANA PLANTATION COOKBOOK by Remy, $4.95 plus S&H
'DAT LITTLE NEW ORLEANS CREOLE COOKBOOK by Remy, $4.95 plus S&H
'DAT LITTLE CAJUN COOKBOOK by Remy, $4.95 plus S&H
I WANT 'DAT CAJUN COOKBOOK by Remy,
        First Copy, $12.95 plus S&H. Each additional copy $11.95 plus S&H

		QUANTITY	TOTAL
I WANT 'DAT CAJUN COOKBOOK by Remy,	First Copy, $12.95	_____	_____
	Each Additional Copy, $11.95	_____	_____
'DAT LITTLE NEW ORLEANS CREOLE COOKBOOK by Remy,	Each Copy, $4.95	_____	_____
'DAT LITTLE LOUISIANA PLANTATION COOKBOOK by Remy,	Each Copy, $4.95	_____	_____
'DAT LITTLE CAJUN COOKBOOK by Remy,	Each Copy, $4.95	_____	_____
SHIPPING AND HANDLING,	First Book, $2.50		_____
SHIPPING AND HANDLING,	Each Additional Book, $1.50		_____
		TOTAL	_____

SHIP TO: NAME_____

UPS ADDRESS_____

CITY_____STATE _____ZIP _____

MAILING ADDRESS _____

CITY_____STATE _____ZIP _____

PHONE _____

❏ PLEASE ADD MY NAME TO YOUR MAILING LIST

Make Checks Payable to:
Remy Laterrade • P.O. Box 3942 • Lafayette, LA 70502 • Do Not Send Cash!